ATLANTA

MODELING INDUSTRY

SECRETS REVEALED

resources for:

child and adult models,
their agents and managers

by
JAWAR

"Know Thyself" Kemetic Proverb

© 2007 JAWAR
ISBN 10 DIGIT: 0-9759380-4-5
ISBN 13 DIGIT: 978-0-9759380-4-1
Library of Congress Control Number: 2006940500

by JaWar

FIRST EDITION

Published by

Music Industry Connection, LLC
P.O. Box 52682, Atlanta, GA 30355, USA
800-963-0949 www.mt101.com questions@mt101.com

Printed in the U.S.A.

The information provided in this book is intended only as a resource guide for aspiring models, agents and modeling managers. Remember to always verify the company and contact names found in this book before submitting material. There are a number of resources needed to achieve success in the business of modeling that are not contained in this book. The authors and publishers have attempted to verify the accuracy of the resources in this book; however, the information provided is subject to change. The authors and publisher disclaim all responsibility for any loss or damages.

Cover Design: Ashil for Designs Apart
Edited by: Seneferu Ast

DEDICATION

This book is dedicated to ignorance that permeates the modeling business. To the men that continuously take advantage of young women hoping to be a shining star in the world of modeling, film and fashion. To unscrupulous modeling agencies that take advantage of unknowing models and their parents. To unprofessional photographers that seek to take advantage of there modeling clients. To the people who thought I would only write books about the music industry.

ACKNOWLEDGEMENTS

I want to thank the Creator and the Ancestors for giving me another opportunity to make a positive difference in someone else's life. To my family for being a mega support unit as I birth yet another book – to Granny for always having something funny to say, to Momma for making me laugh, saying who I shall become and listening, to Baba Moorise for being the best Baba anyone could have, to Pops for demonstrating a serious work ethic, to Big Josh for giving me insight in the world of modeling and to Kiesha for doing her part with the Los Angeles Music Industry Connection Book. Thank you to Nina Albari, Randy, Izlaam, Erikka Tiffani, Nina Spicer, Makeema, Anthony–Cupcake, Inc., Ashil–Desgin Apart, Randy, DJ Bingy, Kevin, Ebony, Hasson Diggs, Jae Davis, Jamese, Lillie-S.I.R. Magazine, Michelle, Quaren, Renee and Tanya Rabb.

TABLE OF CONTENTS

MODEL INTERVIEWS

INTRODUCTION

Writing and publishing the first edition of the Atlanta Modeling Industry: Secrets Revealed has been an exciting and fun learning experience at worse. This book took me out of my comfort zone of the music industry and cast me into a pit of unfamiliarity the modeling business. I often did not know what I did not know I needed to know. I had to remove the brand I built in the music business and start from the ground up in the modeling world. I went to numerous modeling and casting calls, fashion shows and networking parties. Anywhere the modeling industry was I sought to be there as well.

I found that aspiring models are very much like aspiring artists and authors. They seek recognition for their craft and desire to get paid well from their work. Like aspiring artists and authors they often lack the knowledge of the business and how to avoid the pitfalls of the industry. In my humble opinion models have it far worse than artists and authors. Models are judged primarily on the proverbial look and flavor of the month. Their skill is not as the musician, singer or songwriter. You can't hear the melody they create, feel the beat of their drum or listen to words of inspiration, loved loss or social awareness. A models skill is not based on word arrangement or story-telling ability as an author or writers is. A models success on the surface is based primarily on a look. A look that the model has no control over, they either have it at that very moment or they don't. However, in researching for this book I have found a secret formula for a models success in the industry. The secret has very little to do with outer beauty. The secret exists and only reveals itself to those that seek it, to those that desire it, to those that hunger for it. The secret will be revealed in this book, but only to those that have an obsession to obtain it, then and only then will the secret be revealed.

My goal is to provide a how to resource tool, reference guide and directory for models, photographers, make-up artists and talent agencies actively involved in the business and to increase awareness for companies engaged in the Atlanta Modeling Industry. The book is designed to give aspiring models and models new to Atlanta practical steps and tips for achieving their goals and realizing their success. I want to thank God for giving me an angle to publish another book.

GETTING STARTED

WHY DO YOU NEED THIS BOOK?

A successful career in the modeling industry requires sacrifice, hard work, intelligence, having a great team of professionals on your side and being in the right place at the right time. The Atlanta Modeling Industry: Secrets Revealed has practical information and useful contacts that will help you achieve your goals and realize your potential. In addition, the modeling book has the most comprehensive directory of modeling and fashion industries for the Atlanta Market. The book includes names, physical mailing addresses, phone & faxes numbers, websites and email addresses. This book was designed to help you increase your knowledge base and grow the Atlanta Modeling Industry.

Many of the companies in this book may be instrumental in helping you move your career forward faster. Keep in mind that these companies may provide you with valued services and require some financial commitment on your part. Before working with any of the companies listed in this or any other directory remember to verify their references, put all agreements in writing and always follow your instincts. If something is to good to be true, it probably is. Before signing any agreements you will want to retain (hire) the services of a competent entertainment attorney. Later in the book I give details on selecting an attorney and a list of entertainment attorneys in Atlanta.

WHAT ARE MODELING REVENUE STREAMS?

As a model you should always consider the multiple revenue streams that are available to you. They may include video modeling, modeling for fashion & clothing companies, print modeling, endorsing products and/or services, getting into t.v. and film as an actress or actor, voiceovers and a host of other activities to increase your earning potential. I have touched on a few areas below. The most important things are to keep your eyes and ears open for new opportunities, desire to learn more to earn more, create a practical plan and execute that plan like there is no tomorrow.

To ensure your long-term financial success you may want to employ (hire) a tax professional, business manager and financial advisor. Initially, you may not be able to afford the services of these professionals, however, you may educate yourself on the basics of sound investment decision-making. To help you achieve this goal I have included the "Creating Wealth" Section at the end of this book. Do not take this section lightly, for even if you do not achieve the success you desire as a professional model the information in the "Creating Wealth" Section is most beneficial to you no matter what profession you choose.

- **Video models** are those models that appear in music videos. Atlanta has become a hot bed for the music industry, especially for Hip Hop and R&B and often referred to as the third coast of the music industry. The only one true way to become a video model is by networking in the music industry. You could meet newly signed artists who are preparing to shoot their video that want you to do a feature. You might meet an entertainment attorney, manager or video producer who may inform you of a casting call to be in a video. The most important thing is networking so people know you are a model seeking work. *The Atlanta Music Industry Connection: Resources for Artists, Producers & Managers* has the most comprehensive directory of Atlanta Music Business Professionals and will help you make those contacts to expand your network. At the end of this book you will find an order form for getting *The Atlanta Music Industry Connection: Resources for Artists, Producers & Managers* or you may visit www.mt101.com.

- **Modeling clothes** is a fantastic way to build your resume, gain increased exposure and get free apparel. There are a number of new and independent clothing companies and fashion designers in Atlanta who need the services of a professional model, but who may not be able to pay top dollar for the services. As an aspiring model you are in a unique position to offer your professional modeling services for a reduced rate. In exchange for offering your services as a reduced rate you should receive some other form of compensation. You might receive free apparel or clothes from the designer. You may receive a free photo shoot from the designer. Whatever the agreement ensure that you get the contract in writing and have one of the attorneys in this book to look it over for you. I have not seen any one model or models take this concept to new heights in Atlanta. Imagine if you would someone who modeled enough clothes whereas he or she appeared in commercials and most of the print media in the city. That model would get the attention of the public and the industry. That model would truly build their brand. Building your brand is where you position yourself to generate large amounts of money through increased endorsement deals.

- **Print modeling** is similar to modeling clothes. However, you are not focused only on fashion, but other products and services as well. You could model the latest wireless device, internet service provider, car dealership and so forth. You are only limited by your own creativity and networking opportunities. Of course, you will want to ensure that you are paid for your professional modeling services. This way if the company decides not to

run their Ads you still receive compensation for your
work.

- **Endorsing products and/or services** is another way
  to build your resume and earn additional money.
  Endorsing products or services will most likely
  increase as your brand, popularity and look
  increases. Keep in mind that all money may not be
  good money. You want to endorse those products
  that don't compromise your personal, spiritual and
  religious values. When money is tight you may find
  yourself wanting to do things you would not
  ordinarily do. I encourage you to stay true to who
  you are and who you are meant to become. Stay
  the course. It will build your character and force you
  to become more business savvy. To truly position
  yourself to earn money by endorsing products and
  services you must build your brand, you must build
  your brand, you must build your brand. You are
  your brand. Your attitude, look, style and clothes all
  are part of your image and brand that you build. As
  your brand grows in popularity you are in a unique
  position to command top dollar for endorsing
  products and services.

- **From modeling to movies.** Atlanta is a hot bed for
  entrepreneurs in the entertainment community. The
  music industry spearheaded the movement, but
  film, acting, modeling and book publishing have
  begun the independent route as well. Initially, the
  independent route was employed as a way to get

into the major leagues. Now the independent route is an alternative where entrepreneurs in entertainment are making a good living doing what they enjoy doing and have become the major leagues in their own right. As a model in Atlanta you have the opportunity to take advantage of this lively spirit. You can move from print modeling to video modeling to being in movies. There are a number of independent filmmakers and video production companies in Atlanta that frequently seek the services of a professional actor or actress. By increasing your network, being professional and attending casting calls you improve your chances of appearing in many of the movies being shot in Atlanta. To get your feet wet you will want to appear as an extra in feature films. Remember to invest in yourself. You will want to take acting classes and attend workshops on the acting process. You will find yourself having to travel to accomplish these goals by doing so you increase your knowledge base, expand your network and have the opportunity to build your brand.

WHAT IS A MODELING SCHOOL?

A modeling school is an institution that enables aspiring models to learn the needed techniques to improve their chances for long-term success in the business.

I spoke with a number of models that were disappointed with their modeling school experience. In life experiences are what we make out of them. What seems to be consistent among models is that a modeling school will help them get work as a professional model. The reality is a school typically gives you some process or guideline for doing things, some systematic formula for achieving your goals and realizing your potential. Any model reading this book should know that his or her success will have very little to do with what modeling school they attend. Their success will be centered on their positive attitude, confidence level, professionalism, likeability and proverbial look. To truly succeed as a professional model you must desire, plan and execute daily as though there is no tomorrow. You must be consumed with thoughts of success, good health and wealth as a professional model.

HOW DO I CHOOSE A MODELING SCHOOL?

When selecting a modeling school you will want to know what they will teach you, what are the credentials of the institution and its' faculty (staff) and what is the tuition price. You will want to know how long the school has been operating and what successes its prior students have had. For instance, have any of its students secured work in the top ten print publications? Have any of the schools students starred or been featured in major film releases. Have any of the schools students secured any significant product or service endorsement deals?

WHAT MIGHT A MODELING SCHOOL TEACH?

A modeling school should teach you how to speak in public, runway modeling, how to be photogenic and overall professional etiquette. Like any other school a modeling school is a great place to build your network. Keep your eyes and ears open, as there are always opportunities available. A modeling school is not a models ticket to the big leagues. It is merely a stepping-stone and introduction into the world of modeling. Remember that modeling schools generate revenue (money) from paying students. So their focus is on getting paying students to attend their school. If you cannot find an opportunity, create one.

- Barbizon School of Modeling
  P) 404-261-7332
  3340 Peachtree Rd NE #120, Atlanta, GA 30326
  www.barbizonatlanta.com

- Bauder College
  3500 Peachtree Rd NE, Atlanta, GA 30326
  P) 404-237-7573 P) 800-241-3797 P) 404-237-1642

- Bauder College
  384 Northyards Blvd NW #190, Atlanta, GA 30313
  P) 404-237-7573 P) 800-241-3797

- John Casablancas Modeling & Career Center
  1155 Hammond Drive NE, Atlanta, GA 30328
  P) 770-671-9700

- John Robert Powers School System
  1197 Peachtree St., NE Suite 555
  Colony Square Plaza Level Atlanta, GA 30361
  P) 404-877-1155 F) 404-877-0114

www.johnrobertpowers.net
atlanta@jrpowers.net

- Modeling Images Modeling School
  530 North Burgess TR, Alpharetta, GA 30004
  P) 770-919-8285

- Premiere
  3545 Peachtree Industrial Blvd., Suite 2-B
  Duluth, GA 30096 or 30303
  P) 770-232-1882
  www.premieremodelingatl.com

AGENTS, ATTORNEYS AND MANAGERS

MODELING AGENCIES

Modeling agencies help models find work. Many of them nurture the careers of models and help provide additional resources. However, beware that some agencies attempt to keep you in their loop and spend money with their photographer, website designer and so forth with no goal of truly helping you move your career forward. This book should help increase your knowledge on the modeling business and give you a fresh perspective on being in the industry. It will also give you new contacts so you can become more fluid in your networking and building your brand. While the major modeling agencies are in New York and Los Angeles, Atlanta has its own pool of modeling professionals. One of the reasons I wrote this book was to make the Atlanta Modeling Industry more accessible to those who have dreams of being involved in the modeling business. Below is a list of modeling agencies in Atlanta. Some focus on adult models while others on children. If you are new to the modeling business I encourage you to contact all of them and ask intelligent questions. The experience will help you make informed business decisions moving forward. You may also consider interning at one of the agencies in an effort learn more about the industry first hand. By interning you will learn about the business from the inside and have access to a number of industry professionals.

- 2CRUNK.com Models
  3220 Timber Walk Circle, Atlanta, GA 30052
  P) 404-551-6819
  http://2CRUNK.com
  models@2crunk.com

- A-Line Model Marketing & Development
  120 West Wieuca Rd Northwest, Atlanta, GA 30342
  P) 404-459-8933

- About Faces Models and Talent
  3400 Peachtree Rd, Ste 147 Lobby, Atlanta, GA
  P) 404-233-2006 P) 404-233-2007 F) 404-237-2578
  www.aboutfaces.mt
  info@aboutfacesmt.com

- Actor's Scene
  4300 Buford Drive, Suite 12, Buford, GA 30518
  P) 770-904-6646 F) 770-945-7685

- Alpha Model Group
  5600 Roswell Rd NE, Ste N 200, Atlanta, GA 30342
  P) 404-250-9000

- Amanda's Models & Talent
  1813 Iolda Drive, Valdosta, GA 31601
  P) 229-245-1224 C) 229-834-3291
  amandasmodels@aol.com

- Arlene Wilson Management
  887 West Marietta St., Atlanta, GA 30318
  P) 404-876-8555 F) 404-876-9043
  www.arlenewilson.com
  info.atlanta@arlenewilson.com

- Atlanta Models & Talent
  2970 Peachtree Rd NW, Suite 660, Atlanta, GA, 30305
  P) 404-261-9627 F) 404-231-5410

- Atlanta Young Faces Look Model Management
  6075 Roswell Road NE, Suite 118, Atlanta, GA
  P) 404-255-3080
  www.atlantayoungfaces.com

- Atlanta's Young Faces
  359 Johnson Ferry Rd., NE, Atlanta, GA, 30328
  P) 404-255-3080 F) 404-255-3173
  www.atlantayoungfaces.com

- Auston's Professional Modeling
  3400 Peachtree Road NE, Atlanta, GA 30326
  P) 404-233-2006

- Babes & Beaus
  4757 Canton Rd Suite 107 Marietta, GA 30066
  P) 770-928-5832

- Bamm Entertainment
  184 Walker St Sw, Atlanta, GA 30303
  P) 404-521-1188 P) 866-475-2266 F) 404-521-1267
  bamm_entertainment@hotmail.com

- Beauty in a Blink, Model & Talent Management
  595 Piedmont Avenue, NE Suite 320-182
  Atlanta, GA 30308
  P) 404-783-2933 P) 877-321-0200

www.beautyinablink.com
newtalent@beautyinablink.com

- Believe Models & Talent
2055-C Scenic Highway, Suite 199
Snellville, GA 30078
P) 770-962-3580 F) 678-225-7000
www.believemodeltalent.com
info@believemodeltalent.com

- Betty Dinkins Model Agency
Atlanta, GA 30303
P) 404-691-0122

- Bohannon Modeling Agency & Photo Studio
4820 Old National Highway, Atlanta, GA 30337
P) 404-209-0909

- Burns Agency
602 Hammett Dr Decatur, GA 30032
P) 404-299-8114

- Casting by Carolyn
P) 678-571-7480
www.castingbycarolyn

- Catalyst Model Group
275 13th Street Northeast, Atlanta, GA 30309
P) 404-685-9909

- Cick Models
79 Poplar St., Atlanta, GA 30303
P) 404-688-9700

- Click Models of Atlanta, Inc.
84 Peachtree Street, Ste. 400, Atlanta, GA 30303
P) 404-688-9700 F) 404-688-9705
www.clickmodelsatl.com

click@clickmodelsatl.com

- Code Talent Management
  952 Peachtree Street Northeast, Atlanta, GA 30309
  P) 404-873-0407

- Code Talent Management
  2849 Piedmont Rd NE, Atlanta, GA 30305
  P) 404-264-9030
  www.codetalentmanagement.com

- Collective Image Models
  494 North Highland Ave. Northeast, Atlanta, GA 30307
  P) 404-228-8749

- Crossings International Modeling Agency
  1850 Parkway Pl., Suite 420, Atlanta, GA 30067
  P) 770-578-4622 F) 770-509-9034

- Diamond Productions
  1026 Spring Street, Suite 710, Atlanta, GA 30309
  P) 706-333-3779
  www.diamondproductionsmodels.com
  diamondproductions@hotmail.com

- E Glamour Inc
  3545 McCall Place Suite E, Atlanta, GA 30340
  P) 770-234-0080

- Elite Atlanta
  1708 Peachtree St. NW, Suite 210, Atlanta, GA 30309
  P) 404-872-7444 F) 404-874-5266
  www.eliteatlanta.com

- Epiphani
  118 Palmetto Road, Suite-E, Tyrone, GA 30290
  P) 678-364-9099 F) 770-486-1622

- ETMP (Empire Talent Management Promotions)

4047 Holcomb Bridge Rd., Norcross, GA 30093
P) 678-334-9240
www.etmp.biz

- Expressions
P.O. Box 8563, Atlanta, GA 31106
P) 404-872-7276 F) 404-355-7177

- First Step Model & Talent Agency
P.O. Box 1098, Snellville, GA 30078
P) 678-471-5161 F) 770-963-5163
www.firststep-1.com
dw8721@firststep-1.com

- Galaxy Models & Talent
3340 Peachtree Road NE, Atlanta, Georgia 30326
P) 404-261-7332

- Genesis Model & Talent
1465 Northside Dr #120, Atlanta, GA
P) 404-294-6090

- Hop Models and Talent Agency
5825 Glenridge Dr., Suite 2-218, Atlanta, GA 30328
P) 404-297-6638 F) 404-297-6858
www.hopmodels.com
info@hopmodels.com

- Houghton Talent Inc
919 Collier Rd NW, Atlanta, GA 30318
P) 404-603-9454
www.houghtontalent.com

- Jachal Studios
One Galleria Parkway, Suite 1C17, Atlanta, GA 30339
P) 770-951-8898
www.jachalstudio.com

- Kelly Kelly Enterprises, Inc
  10945 State Bridge Rd., Alpharetta, GA 30022
  P) 770-664-2410

- Kidding Around Models and Talent
  1479 Spring St Atlanta, GA 30309
  P) 404-872-8582
  www.kiddinaroundmodels.com

- Marion Webb Agency
  126 B Bankhead Hwy., Carrollton, GA 30117
  P) 404-245-5280
  www.marionwebb.com
  marion@marionwebb.com

- Mark Reed Model Management
  1830 Balmoral Rd Atlanta, GA 30080
  P) 770-444-9731 F) 770-444-9732

- Millie Lewis Savannah
  302 Stephenson Ave., Savannah, GA 31405
  P) 912-354-9525 F) 912-354-9552
  www.millielewissavannah.com
  info@millielewissavannah.com

- Models of Atlanta
  79 Poplar Street, Suite B, Atlanta, GA

- Model Production
  530 North Burgess Trail, Atlanta, GA

- People Store Hot Shot Kids
  2004 Rockledge Road NE, Atlanta, GA 30324
  P) 678-442-0012
  www.peoplestore.net
  talentinfo@peoplestore.net

- Real People Models Talent Inc
  1479 Spring Street NW, Atlanta, Georgia 30309
  P) 404-872-8582
  www.realpeoplemodels.net

- John Robert Powers
  1197 Peachtree St NE, Atlanta, GA 30361
  P) 404-877-1155

- TMA Talent
  1702 Dunwoody Place, Atlanta, GA

- Spicer-Evans Company, LLC
  P.O. Box 1260, Snellville, GA 30078
  P) 770-714-0339
  www.spicerevans.com
  nina.spicer@spicerevans.com

- Suarez Entertainment
  31 South Main St, Atlanta, GA 30303
  P) 404-555-1212

- Tiffany Diamonds Agency
  P) 404-587-4344 P) 678-851-6511

- William Reynolds Agency
  1936 N Druid Hills Rd NE, #101, Atlanta, GA 30319
  P) 404-636-1974
  www.williamreynoldsagency.com

- World Wide Model Group
  120 West Wieuca Road NW, Atlanta, GA 30342
  P) 404-531-0030

- Xcel Talent Agency
  P.O. Box 191731, Atlanta, GA 31119
  P) 404-808-6546 F) 404-634-6909
  www.xceltalent.com

WHAT IS A MODELING AGENCY?

A modeling agency is a company that seeks modeling talent and places that talent with various companies and events for photo shoots, video, commercial, print and runway modeling. Typically, there is a written agreement between the model and the modeling agency. The agreement may or may not be exclusive. With exclusive contracts, models generally are barred from working with other agencies or the agencies corporate clients while under contract. Exclusive contracts are not necessarily a bad thing, but the model should have some written guarantees that the agency will get them work on a recurring basis, since this will be their only source of obtaining video, commercial, print and runway assignments. Whenever I consider an exclusive contract I normally want it to be for the shortest time period possible. I'm also concerned with the options section of the agreement. The options agreement is where automatic extensions may occur to continue the length of the agreement.

Before signing any agreement models should contact one of the entertainment attorneys in this book to get legal advice.

WHEN DO I NEED AN AGENT?

You may need a modeling agent when you are ready to start working professionally as a print, runway, video or commercial model.

While an agents job is to find models work a model should not put their career in the hands of any one agent or single entity. The model should consistently brand, market and promote their professional services. They should regularly seek and attend model and casting calls, networking events, fashion and talent shows and video shoots. As an aspiring model you must aggressively network with the right professionals. Photographers, agents, promotions companies, magazine publishers and other models may all help you achieve certain levels of success as a professional model. The same people you see on your way up are the same people you see on your way down, discount no one, everyone is important.

HOW SHOULD I SELECT AN AGENT?

There are a number of factors you should consider before signing with any agent. Consider how long the agent has been in business, placement of past and current models in various jobs, the agent's reputation in the modeling business and their level of professionalism and common courtesy to you while on the phone and visiting their office. It is not customary in the business for the agent to ask a model to pay any fees. If you are asked to pay for anything by the agent be extremely cautious.

Ask other models what agents they have had a great experience with and what ones they have not. Qualify their response by asking them what made their experience great or not. You may also want to check with the better business bureau or BBB (www.bbb.org) to see if the agency has had any complaints filed against them. There are a few sites that warn models against modeling agencies who have been known to have unscrupulous business dealing. These sites may be found in the websites you need to know section. You may also do a search for dishonest modeling agencies in your favorite search engine on the Internet.

A SPECIAL NOTE ABOUT FEES:

While it is not customary for models to pay a fee to their agency and some agencies have been known to send models to their photographers this is not and all bad thing. The reason I say this is if you are a model you will need photos and comp cards. If you walk into an agency and don't have photos you will need some before they can get you work. If you have photos, but the agency thinks they are not the right ones you may consider taking more photos. The agency should at minimum tell you the type of look they are seeking so you may schedule your own photo shoot if you are not comfortable using the agencies photographer. There are a number of photographers in this book. I would suggest calling as many as you can until you find the person or persons that is best suited to your financial restraints and business etiquette (manners).

Models and their promotions companies have consistently told me photographers may be instrumental in helping models find work. A great photographer will not only be extremely professional and have an eye for pictures, but will be well connected with top agencies and casting companies.

HOW DO AGENTS GET PAID?

Agents get paid a commission on what their clients (models) make. This commission may be anywhere from 5% to 25% of the models gross or net revenue (income). The gross revenue is the amount of money a model generates before taxes. The net revenue is the amount of money a model generates after taxes. Normally, an agency will want to get paid from the models gross revenue since this would be a higher percentage over the net revenue. Flip side the model will want to pay the agency from their net revenue since this would be a lower amount.

Keep in mind that the percentages will play a part in the overall amount as well. At the end of the day it is all about creating a mutually beneficial (win/win) situation for both model and agency.

DO AGENTS NEED A SPECIAL LICENSE?

No, however reputable model and talent agencies will have a business license and often be registered with the secretary of state as either a LLC (limited liability company) or corporation. More often than not agent's offices will be in a commercial building. You may find some from time to time that have a home office. With technology it may be feasible for some agents to have a home office to reduce cost and overhead.

WHERE MAY I FIND AN AGENT?

The best way to find an agent is through a referral, you may use directories such as this one, the Internet, the phone book and from other professionals in the industry. Social networking websites are a great place to meet other modeling professionals. Sites such as Myspace.com or Craigslist.com may be good starting points, but don't stop there, always keep your hand on the pulse to locate more places to network and find agents. Phonebooks are a great starting point for modeling agents if you are in a heavily populated city such as New York or Los Angeles. As Atlanta continues to become an entertainment magnet for music, movies and modeling many companies will have pilot offices and reps here. It may be a good idea to contact New York and Los Angeles and ask if those agencies have contacts in the Atlanta Market. Major phonebooks have an Internet Component that will allow you to search for agencies in various cities. The modeling business is truly a who you know business, attending as many related industry functions is paramount to meeting the right people who will help you advance your career. Perhaps during these events you will meet the persons who know the people who will introduce you to your agent.

WHEN DO I NEED A MANAGER?

That depends on your personality and business savvy. Some people have a knack for networking, are extremely organized, knowledgeable about the modeling business and do well in improving and perfecting their craft. So, in the beginning of your career you may not need the service of a manager. As you become more commercially successful and are asked to make guest appearances and sought after for endorsements, you may seek the services of a qualified manager who would help you navigate your growing success.

You may need the services of a manager in the early stages of your career to help you identify career goals and objectives, develop your craft, network with modeling industry professionals and focus on achieving success.

HOW SHOULD I SELECT A MANAGER?

While there are a number of factors that you should consider before choosing a manager a few include the manager's ability to multi-task, organizational skills, professionalism, knowledge of the business of modeling, extensive industry contact list and believe in you as an modeling. The manager should have some knowledge of contracts, negotiations, how management companies operate and basic bookkeeping and/or accounting skills.

MANAGERS AND POWER OF ATTORNEY

Power of attorney allows someone or entity to negotiate and sign contracts on your behalf. Given someone power of attorney should not be taken lightly. Generally, you would give a management company power of attorney to sign contracts when you may not be available. These contracts will tend to be fairly standard. For instance, you manager or agent may sign an appearance contract in your absence. The agreement may be as basic as stating when, where and what you are to do at a given event. In addition, it will detail how and the amount of money you would receive for the assignment.

Given your management company or agent power of attorney may be a detriment if you grant them ability to sign any agreement in your absence. They may have you committed to a number of engagements that you are not comfortable or in agreement with. You may have already committed to another event and find yourself being double booked. It may be wise not to grant your manager or agent power of attorney unless it is under very limited terms. For example, you may have a clause between you and the management company stating that all agreements signed on your behalf by the management company must first be approved by you via an email or verbal response, preferably an email, because then you have some record of the correspondence.

- Arlene Wilson Model Management
  887 W Marietta St NW Ste #101, Atlanta, GA 30318
  P) 404-876-8555

- Axis Model Management Inc
  120 West Wieuca Road NE, Atlanta, GA 30342
  P) 404-459-0881

- Billboard Models
  277-B East Paces Ferry Rd., Atlanta, 30305
  P) 404-587-5464 F) 404-551-2853
  www.billboardmodels.com
  info@billboardmodels.com

- Click Model Management
  84 Teachtree St., Atlanta, GA 30303
  P) 404-688-9700
  www.clickmodel.com

- Elite Model Management Corporation Atlanta
  1708 Peachtree Street Northwest Suite 210
  Atlanta, GA 30309
  P) 404-872-7444
  www.elitemodel.com

- Genuine Entertainment
  45 Havenwood Lane, Covington, GA 30016
  P) 404-486-3403 F) 770-784-1735
  genuine_entatl@yahoo.com

- Halo Models & Talent
  1900 The Exchange, Suite 408, Atlanta, GA 30339
  P) 770-690-9831
  www.halomanagement.com
  info@halomanagement.com

- Hot Girlz Promotions & Management
  998 Main St., Lake Dr., Stone Mountain, GA 30088

P) 404-558-3036 P) 404-610-2939
www.theheatonline.com
ninaalbari@yahoo.com

- Mark Reed Model Management
  1830 Balmoral Road SE, Atlanta, GA 30303
  P) 770-444-9731

- Slamm Management
  2 Lenox Pointe, Suite C, Atlanta, Georgia 30324
  P) 404.869.5650 P) 404-733- 0501 F) 404 869.5628
  www.slammmanagement.com

- Structure Model Management
  P) 404-914-0346
  structuremodels@yahoo.com

WHAT TYPE OF ATTORNEY SHOULD I SELECT?

As an aspiring or professional model you will want to seek the professional services of an entertainment attorney. You will want to find somcone who works closely in the modeling, film and television industries. Many of the entertainment attorneys found in this book represent a number of talent professionals.

WHEN DO I NEED AN ATTORNEY?

As a professional model you should seek a qualified entertainment attorney before signing any contracts. In many cases if you are a less seasoned or business savvy model you may also seek a qualified entertainment attorney to help negotiate agreements on your behalf. Never sign an agreement simply because the other party says they need the contract ASAP (as soon as possible). This is a sure fire way to have most of your rights assigned to another person or company. Your rights to your professional stage name, likeness or official website may be assigned unknowingly when you quickly sign a contract without having a competent entertainment attorney review it.

HOW SHOULD I SELECT AN ATTORNEY?

That depends on what you hire the attorney to do and your career goals and objectives. As a model you may need contract drafting and negotiation, professional career development and/or contacts to decision makers at modeling agencies, management companies and T.V. & film studios, etc. Different entertainment attorneys may provide one or all of these services. Some practical factors to consider before selecting a entertainment attorney include: how you met the attorney i.e. where they referred to you by a reliable source, the attorneys experience in the modeling industry, your first instinct (gut feeling) about the attorney (which is probably one of the most important factors of selecting an attorney), how much the attorney charges for his/her services and the connections the attorney has in the modeling, fashion and film industries.

Of course, there are other factors that should be considered before selecting the attorney you will hire to work for you, but this should get you started when the time is right.

HOW MUCH DO ATTORNEY FEES COST?

You can expect to pay anywhere from $200/hr to $450/hr for attorney fees. Many attorneys also require a retainer. A retainer is a deposit to the attorney. The retainer amount varies from one attorney to the next. Some retainers are as low as $1,500 while others are as high as $10,000. Here is how the retainer works. If you pay a retainer of $2,000 and the attorney charges $200/hr you would have a credit for 10 hours of legal services with the attorney. Attorneys and other service professionals use retainers to ensure that they are dealing with a serious client. More importantly it ensures that their time is used wisely.

Like many things in life, an attorney's fees are negotiable. It has been my experience that many attorneys are willing to work with aspiring models and creative types, if they see that you are serious about your craft and are willing to stay the course. Many attorneys had to sacrifice to complete their undergrad and law school studies, so they can appreciate the model who also has a plan and passion to succeed as they did. However, make no mistake about it attorneys do charge for their valued services, expertise and consultation. When contacting the attorneys be prepared to make an investment in your future, be prepared to spend some money in legal services to protect your interest as a professional model. Given that you already have an idea for what entertainment attorneys charge it will be no surprise when they quote you a price. If you need the services of an entertainment attorney and don't immediately have the cash necessary you must desire or will into existence the ability to pay for the services. You must have an obsession for success, you must find a way or make one, legally. Creating a desired result, placing on paper plans of action and then working daily toward that desired result will lead to a great result. Below is a list of entertainment attorneys in Atlanta. Make sure you tell them that you found them in the Atlanta Modeling Industry: Secrets Revealed Book by JaWar.

- K5 Keniley Law Firm, LLC
  4610 Peachtree Industrial Blvd, Norcross, GA 30071
  P) 404-933-1157 F) 404-420-2260
  www.k5law.com
  Scott@k5law.com

- Beitchman & Hudson
  Contact: Lee B. Beitchman or Herman Hudson
  215 Fourteenth Street, NW, Atlanta, GA 30318
  P) 404-897-5252 F) 404-897-5677
  www.arts-entertainmentlaw.com
  Hudson@arts-entertainmentlaw.com

- Brison & Associates, LLC
  2100 DeFoors Ferry Rd., #2025, Atlanta, GA 30318
  P) 404-931-3391
  nbrison@comcast.net

- Brock, Clay & Calhoun, P.C.
  49 Atlanta St., Marietta, GA 30060
  P) 770-422-1776 F) 770-426-6155
  brockclay.com

- Charles J. Driebe Jr.
  6 Courthouse Wy, Jonesboro, GA 30236
  P) 770-478-8894 F) 770-478-9606

- Clarke & Anderson
  3355 Lenox Rd., Suite 750, Atlanta, GA 30326-1332
  P) 404-816-9800 F) 404-816-0555

- Cliff Lovette, Esq.
  1800 Peachtree St., NW, Atlanta, GA 30309
  P) 404-355-9000 F) 404-475-0680
  cliff.lovette@lovettegroup.com

- Cohen, Cooper, Estep & Mudder, LLC
  3350 Riverwood Parkway, Suite 2220
  Atlanta, GA 30339
  P) 404-814-0000 F) 404-816-8900
  www.coco-law.tv

- Cherry & Cherry, LLC
  Veda V. Cherry
  383-A Ralph McGill Blvd., Atlanta, GA 30312
  P) 404-880-9262 F) 404-880-0897
  Vedavc1@aol.com

- Dante Marshall, Esq.
  1970 Cliff Valley Wy, Suite 250, Atlanta, GA 30329
  P) 404-320-5212 F) 404-320-5214
  D_marshall@dmentertainmentgroup.com

- Drew M. Jackson
  P) 404-609-9885

- Ewing & Roseberry
  6323 Roosevelt Hwy., Union City, GA 30291
  P) 678-325-5402 F) 678-325-5401
  monicaewingesq@mindspring.com

- Gate City Bar Association
  Post Office Box 1921, Atlanta, GA 30301-1921
  www.gatecitybar.org

- Georgia Lawyers for the Arts
  877 W. Marietta St. NW Suite J-101, Atlanta, GA 30318
  P) 404-873-3911
  gla@glarts.org

- Greenberg Taurig Atlanta, LLP
  The Forum
  3290 Northside Pkwy., Suite 400, Atlanta, GA 30327
  P) 678-553-2100 F) 678-553-2212

- Hewitt, Katz, Stepp & Wright
  Contact: Leron E. Rogers
  Resurgens Plaza, Suite 2610
  945 East Paces Ferry Road, Atlanta, GA 30326
  P) 404-240-0400 F) 404-240-0401
  leron.rogers@mindspring.com

- Holland & Knight LLP
  One Atlantic Center
  1201 W. Peachtree St, NE, Ste 2000, Atlanta, GA 30309
  P) 404-817-8500 F) 404-881-0470

- John F. Christmas Entertainment & Sports Attorney
  P.O. Box 615, Union City, GA 30291
  P) 770-374-8294 F) 770-306-0664
  jochristm@aol.com

- Jonathan E. Leonard, P.C.
  King Plow Arts Center
  949 W. Marietta St., NW, Ste X-102, Atlanta, GA 30318
  P) 404-892-2001 F) 404-892-7001
  jleonard@jellaw.net

- Joseph Arrington II Esq.
  1201 Peachtree St., 400 Colony Sq.,
  Suite 200 Atlanta, GA 30361
  P) 404-870-9082
  jarringtonll@hotmail.com

- Law Offices of Sidney A. Robbins, LLC
  P.O. Box 4079, Atlanta, GA 30302
  P) 404-589-3595 F) 404-589-3594
  srobbinsa@aol.com

- Lopes McKamey-Lopes
  44 Broad St., NW, Suite 501, Atlanta, GA 30303
  P) 404-589-9000 F) 404-832-4120
  firm@lopesmckameylopes.com

- Marvin S. Arrington, Jr.
  775 Houston Mill Rd, Suite #4, Atlanta, GA 30329
  P) 404-633-3396 P) 404-402-4361
  www.arringtonlawfirm.com
  marvin@arringtonlawfirm.com

- Myers & Kaplan Intellectual Property Law, LLC
  The 1899 Building, 1899 Powers Ferry Rd, Suite 310
  Atlanta, GA 30339
  P) 770-541-7444 P) 866-541-7441 F) 770-541-7448
  www.myersiplaw.com

- Neighbors, Lett & Johnson, LLC
  The Candler Building
  127 Peachtree St., Suite 555, Atlanta, GA 30303
  P) 404-653-0881 F) 404-653-1171
  www.neighborslettandjohnson.com
  jlett@neighborslettandjohnson.com

- Nicholson & Associates
  1252 W. Peachtree St., NW, Suite 500
  Atlanta, GA 30309
  P) 404-874-6262

- Omara Harris
  P.O. Box 19199, Atlanta, GA, 31126
  P) 404-409-7354
  gamusiclawyer@aol.com

- Rob Hassett
  990 Hammond Dr., Suite 990, Atlanta, GA 30328
  P) 770-393-0990 F) 770-901-9417
  www.internetlegal.com
  rob@internetlegal.com

- Robert L. Hicks
  1291 Fontaine Ave. SW, Atlanta, GA 30311
  P) 404-753-2820

- Robinson & Morgan
  3355 Peachtree Rd., Suite 500, Atlanta, GA 30326
  P) 404-995-7060 F) 404-995-7001

- Self, Glass & Davis
  The Platinum Tower
  1455 Lincoln Pkwy., Suite 300, Atlanta, GA 30346
  P) 770-563-9300 F) 770-563-9330

- Shuli L. Green
  P.O. Box 2839, Decatur, GA 30031
  P) 404-222-8411
  shuligreen@yahoo.com

- Standford, Fagant & Giolito
  1401 Peachtree St., NE, Suite 238, Atlanta, GA 30309
  P) 404-897-1000 F) 404-897-1990

- Stephanie S. Kika
  8108 Trolley Sqxing NE, Atlanta, GA 30306
  P) 770-664-9262 F) 770-892-2150

- Stokes & Murphy
  3593 Hemphill St., Atlanta, GA 30337
  P) 404-766-0076 F) 404-766-8823
  mail@stokesnmurphy.com

- Vernon Slaughter
  1741 Commerce Drive, Atlanta, GA 30318
  P) 404-355-2755 F) 404-355-2720
  slaughterv@bellsouth.net

- Vince Phillips
  P.O. Box 20084, Atlanta GA 30325
  P) 404-522-8000 F) 404-522-7643

- Washington Law Firm
  Contact: Karl Washington
  1353 Cleveland, East Point, GA 30344
  P) 404-768-3963 F) 404-768-3966
  karlwashington@att.net

- Weiznecker, Rose, Mattern & Fisher, P.C.
  1800 Peachtree Street, NW
  Suite 620 Atlanta, GA 30309
  P) 404-365-9799 F) 404-917-0979
  www.wrmflaw.com

CASTING CALLS & PHOTO SHOOTS

WHAT IS A CASTING CALL?

A casting call is simply an interview for a commercial, movie, stage play or music video, etc. It is where talent reads from a script, answers questions or performs other professional tasks presented by the casting company. Casting calls may last a few minutes or a few days depending on the size and budget of the project. For larger casting calls presented by a major film company or television station lines are typically extremely long and will require you to be there all day just to read the pre-written script. The script itself is normally short lived and you either make the cut for the next audition or reading or you don't. More than likely you will have to go on many casting calls before you make the cut for a new show, stage play, model gig and so forth. You will need to have a heart of a lion to succeed as a model. The magazines, movies and television don't give you the real deal on the entertainment business. It is extremely competitive, often cut throat and very intense only those willing and able to quickly adapt and overcome have a chance for rising above the rest. If this does not sound like your personality, do yourself a favor and forward this book to someone else.

HOW CAN I PREPARE FOR A CASTING CALL?

You should find out as much information about a particular casting call as possible. Truth be told your preparation may often be minimal. You typically go in with all your prior experiences and education, but at the end of the day the casting director has an idea for what they are looking for. If you have the goods you're in.

WHAT SHOULD A PHOTOGRAPHER DO?

Take pictures for comp cards and portfolios. Remember to know what you want from your photographer; getting all quotes in writing before beginning any photo session conveys your expectations. Photo sessions may run over the original time allotted, always ask what are the rates incase your session runs over the estimated time. You will want to use reputable photographers. One of the best ways to find a reputable photographer is by asking other models whom they have used.

A photographer who is actively involved in the modeling, music and entertainment industries may be able to plug you into a larger network of working professionals. This type of networking can't be overstated. While most the contacts in this book are for Atlanta you may use the methods mentioned for finding a professional photographer in any market. Below is a list of professional photographers in Atlanta. Remember to tell them that you found their contact information in the Atlanta Modeling Industry: Secrets Revealed Book by JaWar.

- Allwyn Forrestor Photography
  1869 Clay Drive, Suite 1, Marietta, GA 30064
  P) 404-502-0745
  Allwyn_forrestor@yahoo.ca

- Arial Productions
  2404 Huntingdon Chase, Atlanta, GA 30350
  P) 770-394-9392 F) 404-394-8285
  greggcoyle2000@yahoo.com

- Arnaz Photography
  706 McKoy Street, Decatur, GA 30030
  P) 404-210-8889 F) 770-446-1073

- A Salett Music & Film Co.
  165 Ridge Ave., NW, Atlanta, GA 30318
  P) 404-668-7677
  Theproducer0007@yahoo.com

- A Touch of Class Photography
  6830 Roswell Rd., 1E, Atlanta, GA 30328
  P) 404-795-9195
  www.atouchofclassphotography.com
  info@atouchofclassphotography.com

- Bess Holder Photography
  7500 Roswell Road, #70, Atlanta, GA 30350
  P) 404-931-0005
  www.bessholder.com

- Bill Lisenby
  527 Trabery Ave., NW, Atlanta, GA 30309
  P) 404-874-7921

www.billlisenby.com
bill@billlisenby.com

- Bob Mahoney Photography
  4449 Parkspring Terrace, Norcross, GA 30092
  P) 404-949-9431
  www.bobmahoney.com

- Bobi Dimond Creative Photography
  4086 Columns Drive, Marietta, GA 30067
  P) 770-937-0007

- Calvin Lockwood Photography
  211 Peters Street, Atlanta, GA 30313
  P) 404-221-0201
  www.calvinlockwood.com
  calvin@calvinlockwood.com

- Chris Hamilton Photography
  652 Bellemeade Ave NW, Atlanta, GA 30318
  P) 404-355-9411
  www.hamphoto.com
  rita@hamphoto.com

- Collective Image Models & Photography
  Atlanta, Georgia 30318
  P) 404-609-7022 P) 404-412-3548
  joshuakniselycollectiveimagemodels.com

- CW Design & Photo
  Atlanta, GA 30303
  (404) 284-1230

- D2K Models Design Group
  2230 Leicester Way, Atlanta, GA 30316
  P) 404-441-5794
  www.d2kmodels.com
  moussa@d2kmodels.com

- D&G Enterprise
  P.O. Box 49692, Atlanta, GA 30329
  P) 404-633-6825
  www.dandgenterprise.biz
  l_dear@dandgenterprise.biz

- Dan McCain
  4459 D Hwy 120, Duluth, GA 30097
  P) 770-853-2909
  www.danmccainproductions.com

- Diamond Photography
  P.O. Box 638, Redan, GA 30074
  P) 770-354-6378
  www.theultimatediamondmine.com

- DiVitale Photography
  1735 DeFoor Place NW, Atlanta, GA 30318
  P) 404-350-7888
  www.divitalephoto.com
  jim@divitalephoto.com

- Drexina A. Nelson
  P.O. Box 4294, Atlanta, GA 30303
  P) 404-438-2595
  dnelson@stylonline.com
  www.drexinanelson.com

- Ed C. Thompson Photography
  2241 Spring Creek Road, Decatur, GA 30033
  P) 404-636-7258 C) 404-375-7616

- Foto Illusion Studios
  2275 Northwest Parkway, Suite 115 Marietta, GA 30067
  P) 678-990-5211
  www.fotoillusion.com

- Garcia Studio Inc.
  933 Fielder Avenue, NW, Atlanta, GA 30318
  P) 404-892-2334
  www.garciastudio.com
  carlo@garciastudio.com

- Haigwood Studios Photography
  565 S. Atlanta Street, Roswell, GA 30075
  P) 770-594-7845
  www.haigwoodstudios.com

- Holidayshots Photography
  3535 Peachtree Rd., Suite 520-151, Atlanta, GA 30326
  P) 404-518-0990
  www.holidayshots.com
  photographer@holidayshots.com

- Jason Ivany Photography
  1280 Woodland Ave., SE, Atlanta, GA 30316
  P) 678-923-8020
  www.jasonivany.com
  Jason@jasonivany.com

- Josh Swain Photography
  2262 Ashley Falls Lane, Suwanee, GA 30024
  P) 770-513-4062

- John Crooms Photography
  2385 Headland Dr., East Point, GA 30344
  P) 404-762-1032 C) 678-612-1064
  www.johncroomsphotography.com
  john@johncroomsphotography.com

- Jon Michael Kownacki Photography
  P.O. Box 5681, Atlanta, GA 31107
  P) 404-288-1224 C) 404-808-2755

- JWJ Photography
  2975 Headland Dr., Atlanta, GA 30331
  P) 404-783-0041

- Kenny's Photography
  1729 Rogers Ave. SW, Atlanta, GA 30310
  P) 404-758-7301 C) 404-247-2018

- Kirk Kingsbury Photography
  2135 Defoor Hills Road, Suite E, Atlanta, GA 30318
  P) 404-352-3675

- Laser Photographics
  290 Hilderbrand Dr., Suite B-9, Atlanta, GA 30328
  P) 404-531-0555 F) 404-531-0044
  www.laserphotographics.com
  laserphotgraphics@mindsping.com

- Lee Marshall Photography
  P) 404-521-3191
  www.leemarshallphotography.com

- Lynda Green Photography
  454 Irwin Street, Atlanta, GA 30312
  P) 404-577-2300 F) 404-577-8576

- Matteblack Photography
  P.O. Box 450327, Atlanta, GA 31145
  P) 770-722-0595 F) 770-939-2256

- Michael Allenberg Photography
  49 Candler Road, NE, Atlanta, GA 30317
  P) 678-641-2914
  www.allenbergphoto.com
  michael@allenbergphoto.com

- Mirror M-Edge Photography
  P.O. Box 92279, Atlanta, GA 30314

P) 404-808-6533 F) 404-3280-0730
www.mirrorimagephotos.com
dj_ol_e@hotmail.com

- Nelda Mays Photography
  P.O. Box 33676, Decatur, GA 30033
  P) 404-499-9700
  www.neldamaysphoto.com
  nelda@neldamaysphoto.com

- Paul Hultberg Photography
  660 9th Street, NW Studio F, Atlanta, GA 30318
  P) 404-817-7055 F) 404-817-9384

- Peter Winkel Photography
  185 Andover Drive, Atlanta, GA 30004
  P) 770-754-3100
  www.peterwinkel.com
  pete@peterwinkel.com

- Photomax
  3375 Buford Hwy, Suite 1020, Atlanta, GA 30329
  P) 404-320-1494 F) 404-320-6291
  www.photomax1hr.com
  photomax@aol.com

- Portfolios for Less
  1836 Westwood Ave, SW, Atlanta, GA 30310
  P) 404-452-3589 P) 404-626-9576
  Portfolios4less@yahoo.com

- Prime Phocus Photography
  P.O. Box 94043, Atlanta, GA 30377
  P) 770-329-2181
  www.primephocus.com
  donnapermell@yahoo.com

- Primetime
  P.O. Box 49531, Atlanta, GA 30359
  P) 404-731-2343
  www.primetimeatlanta.com

- Robin Henson Photographs
  25 4th Avenue, NE, Atlanta, GA 30317
  P) 404-377-5062 C) 404-247-5062

- Ron McDonald
  P) 404-815-1566

- Scott Warhurst Photography
  627 Radford Circle, Atlanta, GA 30188
  P) 404-630-9474
  www.scottwarhurst.com
  scott@scorrwarhurst.com

- Sean Cokes Photography
  650 Hamilton Ave., Studio Z, Atlanta, GA 30312
  P) 404-622-7733
  www.seancokes.com
  scokesphoto@yahoo.com

- Sparkman Photo, Inc.
  Loft 301, 161 Mangum Street, SW, Atlanta, GA 30313
  P) 404-659-0200
  www.sparkmanphoto.com
  clif@sparkmanphoto.com

- Steve Thornton Photography
  P.O. Box 669125, Marietta, GA 30066
  P) 404-231-9900
  www.stevethornton.com
  steve@stevethornton.com

- Studio Prime Time
  P.O. Box 49531, Atlanta, GA 30359

P) 404-843-0999
www.studioprimetime.com
info@studioprimetime.com

- Tanner Griffith Photography
  835 Mid Boradwell Road, Alpharetta, GA 30004
  C) 678-637-4089

- Tshanti Photography Studio
  300 MLK Jr. Dr., SE #144, Atlanta, GA 30312
  P) 678-768-4647
  tshantphoto@hotmail.com

- Upscale Images
  P.O. 2585, Decatur, GA 30031
  P) 770-496-4393 Cell) 678-592-0129
  www.upscale-images.com
  upscale_images@msn.com

- Von Hoene Photography
  500 Bishop Street, Suite B-1, Atlanta, GA 30318
  P) 404-355-4422

- Woodie Williams Photography
  1078 Moores Mill Road, NW, Atlanta, GA 30327
  P) 404-367-0558

- Zach Wolfe Photography
  Studio Nine-Hundred
  900 Dekalb Ave., NE, Atlanta, GA 30307
  P) 404-788-4025
  www.zachwolfe.com
  zach@zachwolfe.com

WHEN DO I NEED A MAKE UP ARTIST?

You will need a make up artists before any professional shoot, appearing on TV or attending a major networking event. A professional shoot could be for print modeling, appearing in a music video or on television. While make up is just that, make up is used to cover something up, while cosmetics should be used to enhance one's natural beauty not cover it up. You will want to use a make up artist before attending any major networking event. This will ensure that your look is consistent.

HOW SHOULD I SELECT A MAKE UP ARTIST?

You will want to select a make up artist on a number of criteria. This is in no particular order. You will want to select them based on the quality of work, their professionalism, competitive pricing and referral. The make up artist should have a portfolio or website highlighting their work history.

HOW MUCH DO MAKE UP ARTIST CHARGE?

Make up artist charge anywhere from $35/hr to $150/hr. Depending on the job, some makeup artist may prefer to get paid by the hour while others may prefer to get paid per project. Getting paid by the hour insures that the makeup artist time is well spent. Meaning they are not at a video or photo shoot for, say 14 hours, but actually only work four of those 14 hours. If the project is big enough the makeup artist may estimate with a great degree of certainty the amount of time it will take to complete a project and find it of better interest to get paid a flat fee. At the end of the day it is all business and negotiable.

57

WHO PAYS THE MAKE UP ARTIST?

Typically, if a model is hiring a make up artist they will pay for the service. As an aspiring model you will need comp cards and professional photographs to include in your portfolio and website, as such you would pay for theses services. If you have been contracted for print, runway or Internet work the person hiring you would typically pay the make up artist fees.

- Bodyworks
  P) 404-816-0989 C) 404-693-0012

- Celeste Lipsey
  P) 404-643-4834

- Erika Mitchell
  P) 404-797-1631 F) 404-344-8146

- Gary Shaw
  P) 404-434-2628

- Heather Tiedeman
  P) 404-797-5583

- Jana Evans
  P) 770-560-4088

- Kat Flynt
  P) 770-365-2855

- Kendra Roseberry
  P) 678-592-2976

- Kian Johnson
  P) 404-468-7630

- Lashawnda German
  P) 888- 623-3877

- Lisa Pettiford-Walker
  P) 404-285-4930

- Marcella Wallin
  P) 770-315-1484

- Melinda Mine'
  P) 678-517-3688

- Nancy Hancock
  P) 678-613-5006

- Nayetta Roby
  P) 770-845-2984 F) 770-987-8167

- Patsy Barile
  P) 678-372-2956

- Paula Molinari-Kent
  P) 404-771-2154

- Platinum Faces
  P) 404-243-7623

- Prosperity International Studios
  P) 404-325-3065 P) 678-933-8939

- Quarean "Nina" Gray
  P) 678-478-8621

- Reese Williams
  P) 404-421-5948

- Rob
  P) 678-886-7391

- Scott Kelly
  P) 678-468-1805

- Terri L. Curtis
  P) 404-228-0464 F) 404-286-8494

- Toni Acey
  P) 678-662-6692

- Yolanda
  P) 678-373-1233

IMAGE CONSULTANTS & FASHION STYLISTS

- It Factor
  2936 F North Druid Hills Rd., Atlanta, GA 30329
  P) 404-849-4062 P) 404-849-1747
  www.itfactorconsultants.com
  kellymarie@itfactorconsultants.com

- Mink Image Consulting
  P) 770-845-2984 F) 770-987-8167
  www.minkimage.com

- Styles by Maxx
  P) 800-310-2636 P) 404-246-9394
  stylesbymaxx@yahoo.com

- Teon Gooden
  P) 404-219-1862 P) 678-525-6444
  www.jaeluvle.com

- Trend Setterz
  2020 Howell Mill Rd., Suite C-124, Atlanta, GA 30318
  P) 678-591-4618
  Trendstylist1@aol.com

FASHION SHOW PRODUCTION COMPANIES

- AKA Productions
  P) 404-457-3298
  www.aka-productions.com
  ahaffner@aka-productions.com

- Auroura Productions, Inc.
  3316-A South Cobb Drive, #252, Smyrna, GA 30080
  P) 800-444-0631
  www.aurouraproductions.com
  director@aurouraproductions.com

- Streetwise Production Company, Inc.
  468 NE Blvd., Suite #102, Atlanta, GA 30308
  P) 678-368-2595
  streetwisepc@hotmail.com

WHAT SHOULD I SUBMIT TO A MAGAZINE?

It is a fantastic idea to contact the magazine before submitting any material. Remember most material will not be returned and becomes the property of the magazine; never send your only or original press/media kit. Every magazine will have specific guidelines for submitting material. They will typically request professional photos, a typed written bio or comp cars and contact details. Contact details means your name, phone number, email address, website, physical mailing address and agent or management company that may represent you. Because of the number of characters in the entertainment business, I would suggest getting a post office box instead of giving your home mailing address. You may get a post office box at your local United States Post Office. Getting the smallest box will be the most economical route.

WHAT MAGAZINES SHOULD I TARGET?

You will want to target those magazines that pay the bills and best represent the message that you are attempting to convey. You will want to be mindful of the long-term effects of appearing in adult related magazines may have on your professional modeling, acting or political career. Depending on your look and target audience you will want to focus your efforts on independent music and entertainment publications that feature amateur and aspiring models. Some of the magazines pay the models while others do not. At the end of the day it's about your perceived value in the market place and how you handle your business that ultimately determines if and what you get paid for print work. Whatever the agreement always remember to get it in writing and have your entertainment attorney review your contracts before signing them.

GETTTING A MAGAZINE FEATURE

As an aspiring model you will want to build your print portfolio by appearing in as many tasteful publications as possible. Remember you never know who will be viewing these magazines. In addition, with every photo shoot you should work on improving your overall professionalism and presence. Below is a list of Atlanta Magazines that feature aspiring and professional models. Tell the magazines you found them in the Atlanta Modeling Industry Book by JaWar

- Atlanta Peach
  One Buckhead Plaza
  3060 Peachtree Rd., Suite 1890, Atlanta, GA 30305
  P) 404-494-9669

- Atlanta Talent Magazine
  P.O. Box 28934, Atlanta, GA 30358
  P) 866-853-8539
  www.atlantatalentmagazine.com
  talent@atlantatalentmagazine.com

- AUC Magazine
  100 10th Street NW, Suite 109, Atlanta, GA 30309
  P) 404-961-5700 F) 404-961-1564
  www.aucmagazine.com
  info@aucmagazine.com

- Bovanti Magazine
  4820 Old National Highway, Atlanta, GA 30337
  P) 404-209-0909
  www.bovanti.com

- Fresh Faces Magazine
  3601 Piedmont Rd., Suite 1209, Atlanta, GA 30305
  P) 404-484-4284
  www.freshfacesmagazine.com
  hushpublications@yahoo.com

- Grip Magazine
  684 Antone St., Suite 109, Atlanta, GA 30318
  P) 404-352-4920 F) 404-609-7349
  www.grpmag.com

- Imodel Magazine
  950 Eagles Landing Parkway, Box 304

Stockbridge, GA 30281
P) 678-318-1851 Ext. 102
www.imodelmagazine.com
marshall.smith@imodelmagazine.com

- **OMIGAWD**
  P.O. Box 2124 Smyrna, GA 30081
  P) 678-464-5374 F) 770-463-2590
  www.omigawdmag.com
  darealsafado@yahoo.com

- **Rise Music Magazine**
  P.O. Box 1375, Buford, GA 30515
  www.risemusicmag.com

- **RML Magazine**
  P) 404-437-2142
  www.rmlmagazine.com
  rmlmagazine@yahoo.com

- **Rolling Out Urbanstyle Weekly**
  257 Spring St. SW., Atlanta, GA, 30303
  P) 404-681-2001 F) 404-475-1122
  www.rollingout.com
  info@rollingout.com

- **Smart & Sexy Magazine**
  P.O.Box 2461, Atlanta,GA 30301
  P) 678-437-5007
  www.smartandsexymag.com
  Sophia@smartandsexymag.com

- **S.I.R. (Southeast Independent Report)**
  P) 678-683-4334

- **Talent Scout Magazine**
  3425 Saint James Court, Kennesaw, GA 30152
  P) 770-514-0074 F) 854-264-6631

www.talentscoutmagazine.com
tommivalentino@talentscoutmagazine.com

- Upscale
  600 Bronner Brothers Way, Atlanta, GA 30310
  P) 404-758-7467 F) 404-755-9892
  www.upscalemag.com

WHEN SHOULD I MAKE MY OWN WEBSITE?

You should develop a website as soon as you have a clear focus or road map for your modeling and acting career. At a minimum your site should have a few basic elements. The site should have a bio page, a photo gallery page, an events page-showing your future appearances, a contact page and a merchandise page. Remember that as a model, actor or actress you are a company and brand. You should begin selling t-shirts, coffee mugs and calendars, etc. with your brand (image/face/likeness) on them. This will help you build your brand, market yourself and generate money to pay for your site.

Buy your own domain/url/website name. You should register your own name to ensure that no one else can use it. Many website developers will offer to register your domain name, while this is a value added service I strongly suggest you resist the temptation and register your own domain name. You will simply need access to the Internet and a credit card to process the transaction. Below are a few websites where you may register your own domain name.

- www.buydomains.com

- www.godaddy.com
- www.myrealebiz.com
- www.networksolutions.com
- www.omnis.com
- www.yahoo.com

HOW MUCH WILL I PAY FOR MY WEBSITE?

Having your own website developed may vary from free to ten of thousands of dollars. However, a basic site should cost you know more than a few hundred dollars.

MAY I GET A WEBSITE FOR LESS MONEY?

There are few ways to reduce the cost of having your website developed. First, you can learn how to develop your own website by learning HTML, Flash or some other application. This may take a great deal of time and patience, why bother. Second, you could ask a friend or relative to design the site for you in exchange for a cookie or something corny like that. Better yet you could sell your pictures, t-shirts, coffee mugs, and autographed posters with your face on them for money. You could also sell advertising on your site and share the revenue with your friend or relative. Be sure to get details of your agreement in writing. Specify the terms of the contract, the start and end date and the expectations of everyone involved. I have listed several entertainment attorneys in Atlanta that can help create a workable contract to keep everything nice a business like. Third, find a high school or college student who would design your site in exchange for getting exposure, experience and the opportunity to build their professional website design portfolio. This is my favorite because you are helping someone help themselves while helping yourself at the same time. To find a college student you may have to put flyers up around campus or look for college students on social websites like facebook.com or myspace.com. In any event the experience should be one to remember and help you learn more about marketing and promotions. Who knows you may even meet more people through the process who will help propel your modeling career forward faster.

WHAT IS A COMP OR ZED CARD?

A comp (composite) or zed card normally is double-sided the size being 5.5" X 8.5". Some comp cards may be a little smaller or larger. Call the modeling agencies, schools and photographers in this book and ask them what is the preferred comp card size and why. The comp card has about five different shots (looks) of the model and is used to get work. The card should have contact details for the model. This may include a phone and fax number, email and website or physical mailing address. A model should never leave the house without their comp and business cards. After every business meeting or interview you will want to ask if you may leave one or two of your comp cards with the individual(s).

WHEN DO I NEED A COMP OR ZED CARD?

You will need a comp or zed card immediately upon seeking work as a professional model. A comp card is a models quick photography resume or portfolio.

WHERE DO I GET A COMP OR ZED CARD?

There are several pages with photographers and printers in this book. Anyone of these professionals should be able to help you get zed cards printed or point you in the right direction of someone that does. Some of the photographers in the book may not specialize in the modeling industry and may not be familiar with a comp card, don't be discouraged simply keep asking until you find someone who does. Remember to price compare to ensure you are getting the biggest bang for your buck before getting your cards printed. In the printing business price is not always synonymous with quality. Often times models pay a premium for comp cards simply because they do not know of more economical printers. I've done some of the homework for you by listing a number of printers in the Atlanta Market. Truth be told if you look long enough you may find other printers outside of Atlanta that offer vary competitive pricing. However, I would encourage you to use local printers whenever possible. It ensures the local economy is able to sustain and grow. This is great for all of us, which is one of the reasons I wrote the book in the second place.

HOW MUCH DO COMP CARDS COST?

Comp cards may be priced anywhere from fifty to a few hundred dollars, depending on size, paper quality and the number printed. Generally, the more of something you get made, in this case the more cards are printed the fewer the cost per card (unit). You should pay less per card if you got 1,000 cards made versus if you had 500 cards made. Below is a list of printers in Atlanta that may print your comp cards. By the time you read this book there will undoubtedly be more printers to choose. Always, always, always search for company's competitors. Do business with people that do business with you, treat you fair and are competitively priced. Remember to tell the printing company's below you found them in the Atlanta Modeling Industry: Secrets Revealed Book by JaWar.

- Associated Printing
  5164 Highway 278, NE, Covington, GA 30014
  P) 770-784-9566 F) 770-784-9366

- Canterbury Press
  120 Interstate North Parkway East, Suite 200,
  Atlanta, GA 30339
  P) 770-952-8309 F) 770-952-4623

- Claxton Printing Co.
  408 Woodward Ave., SE, Atlanta, GA 30312
  P) 404-521-0933 F) 404-688-5446
  www.claxtonprinting.com
  jim@claxtonprinting.com

- Corporate Printers
  2195 Pendley Road, Cumming, GA 30041

P) 404-881-3855 F) 404-873-2501

- Digiprint
  2395 Pleasantdale Rd., Suite 4-B, Atlanta, GA 30340
  P) 770-368-2060 F) 770-368-9943

- DocuGraphix, Inc.
  1646 Collingwood Drive, SE, Marietta, GA 30067
  P) 770-217-3628
  www.docugraphix.com
  customer.service@docugraphix.com

- Envision Printing
  1266 Kennestone Cir, Suite 105, Marietta, GA 30066
  P) 678-355-6748 F) 678-355-6637
  www.envisionprinting.com
  cs@envisionprinting.com

- Extreme Media
  1440 Dutch Valley Pl., Suite 945, Atlanta, GA 30324
  P) 404-815-0553 F) 404-815-0314
  www.extremeatlanta.com

- Fletcher Press
  4808 Buford Hwy., Norcross, GA 30071
  P) 770-449-3555 F) 770-449-0535

- Gazelle Printing & Consulting
  20 Executive Park Dr., Ste 2002, Atlanta, GA 30329
  P) 404-320-6926 Cell) 404-454-0668 F) 404-320-5450
  www.gazelleprinting.com
  dalegriffin@gazelleprinting.com

- Imagers
  1575 Northside Drive, Bldg 400, Suite 490,
  Atlanta, GA 30318
  P) 404-351-5800 P) 800-232-5411 F) 404-351-9020
  www.imagers.com

- Image Link
  1379 Chattahoochee Ave., Atlanta, GA 30318
  P) 404-605-0400 F) 404-605-0464
  www.imagelink.net
  staff2@imagelink.net

- Industry Outlet
  684 Antone St. Suite 105, Atlanta, GA 30318
  P) 404-417-9777 P) 877-417-9777 F) 404-759-2072
  print@theindustryoutlet.com

- Inkling Print and Design
  2483 E Briarcliff Rd., Atlanta, GA 30329
  P) 678-388-9662 F) 404-759-2154
  www.inklingprint.com
  info@inklingprint.com

- JPEG Graphics
  2140 Peachtree Rd., NW, Suite 325, Atlanta, GA
  P) 404-214-5001
  www.printinginatlanta.com
  info@printinginatlanta.com

- Kudzu Graphics
  1835 MacArthur Blvd., Atlanta, GA 30318
  P) 404-350-9776 F) 404-350-9554

- Markstarr Multimedia
  644 Antone St., Suite 5, Atlanta, GA 30318
  P) 404-603-9111 P) 888-339-7892 F) 678-999-0467
  www.msgmedia.com
  mark@msgmedia.com

- Small Business Promotions, Inc.
  P.O. Box 1348, Redan, GA 30074
  P) 678-886-8792 P) 770-557-0938
  www.designsnprint.com
  orders@designsnprint.com

- Star Shooters
  277-B East Paces Ferry Rd, Atlanta, GA 30305
  P) 404-869-8844 F) 404-869-8833

- Southern Stamp & Stencil
  428 Edgewood Ave., Atlanta, GA 30312
  P) 800-241-0985 P) 404-522-4431 F) 404-522-4507
  www.southernstamp.com
  info@southernstamp.com

- The Print Shop
  312 Mall Boulevard, Savannah, GA 31406
  P) 912-354-6004
  www.theprintshop.com
  info@theprintshop.com

- Velocity Print & Print Company
  208 Harralson Ave., Atlanta, GA 30307
  P) 404-524-4435

DO I HAVE TO TAKE MY CLOTHES OFF?

You should only take off your clothes when you are comfortable doing so. A legitimate company will not front like they are on the up and up and get you to a video or photo shoot and request that you take off your clothes without informing you before hand. For example, they will tell you that there are nude scenes for the shoot. I would always advise that a woman model go with someone to a casting call, model or video shoot, etc. Attempt to get as many details as possible about any particular shoot. Being forewarned and prepared will increase your chances for success in any environment. Follow some golden rules of life. For instance, if it seems to good to be true it probably is. If your gut, third eye, God Sense is telling you something is not right, it probably is not. Remember to always trust your better judgment. You do not have to take your clothes off to be a professional model. However, when you look at the top 10% of model earners through the years ask yourself if they had to do any nude modeling during the initial stages of their career. If you find that most if not all the model earners in the top 10% had to do nude shoots during the initial stages of their career it may be an indication that you will have to do the same to get to that top position. However, you should never compromise your value and personal belief system for anyone at anytime.

CREATE A SITUATION

When Rap Music first came on the scene many smart, rich and influential people in the music business thought it was just a passing fad. Some thirty years later Rap Music & Hip Hop Culture has entrenched itself within Popular American & World Culture. Hip Hop has become a multi-billion dollar a year industry and currently sees no sign of letting up. One of the reasons for this phenomenon is that in its infancy Hip Hop had to count on itself to move forward. It created a sub-culture of music business professionals. It networked within itself. It created opportunities and situations where people started making money and businesses started to grow. The Hip Hop Culture is a dynamic of the entrepreneurial spirit. It is in fact the American Dream. It has made many millionaires and soon billionaires. Many are making a great living because of the Hip Hop Culture and it's music.

I would encourage models in Atlanta and any market outside of New York and Los Angeles to follow the same spirit of Hip Hop's Infancy. The modeling industry should have regular events where models and other professionals come to learn and network about the business. Models should band together where they have networks to inform each other of various model and casting calls. On the surface this may appear to be informing your competition and to some degree it might. However, if you keep with the bigger picture what you'll find is when you help someone else you will help yourself. There are very few if any organizations designed to look out for the best interest of models, for now models are commissioned with doing the job themselves. Remember, if there is no organization to join, start one.

Recordings artists, producers, managers, singers, songwriters and entertainment attorneys all have organizations they can join to help nurture their careers, models should have the same. Perhaps this book could be the focal point for starting such an organization. You could invite all of the models you know to an open forum to discuss the information in this book. Discuss the pros and cons of this text. Add to the contacts I have listed. Share what other details not mentioned in this book you would like to see in future editions. By using this text as the focal point you give other models a common reason to come together and learn and network with each other. If this event becomes a monthly discussion other modeling professionals such as entertainment attorneys, modeling schools, photographers, website designers, agents and so forth will want to attend in an effort to get your business. What happens at this point is you create a sub-culture of independent thinkers in the modeling industry. Those people start to do business with each other, monies are exchanged and now you position models to grow from the Atlanta Market to a regional, national and international market just as the independent music and film industries have begun to do. Through these monthly meetings new models may find mentors, so that they can avoid some of the pitfalls of the industry. I have provided the resource and creative thought to get you started, but you must continue in good spirit after reading this book. You must create a vision for your success and long-term growth potential in the modeling business, write down your plans and execute relentlessly. There is no time to waste, begin right away or face the reality that keeps most people poor and pitiful, the reality of procrastination.

WEBSITES YOU NEED TO KNOW

Remember the Atlanta Modeling Industry: Secrets Revealed Book is only a stepping-stone for aspiring models, their parents, agents and modeling management companies. There is vast information, contacts and resources at your disposal. I highly recommend increasing your education on the modeling industry through research, networking and reading. To increase your chances for success and long-term growth potential you must desire that thing that you want, create a practical plan and put it in writing then take action daily to make your plan a reality. You must be obsessed with success, good health and wealth. The sites below may be of interest to you and should only be a continuation of your overall learning process about the business of modeling. Always verify sources of information for their validity.

- ➢ www.americamodels.com
- ➢ www.eliteatlanta.com
- ➢ www.ezedcard.com
- ➢ www.fordmodels.com
- ➢ www.howtomodel.com
- ➢ www.imodelmagazine.com
- ➢ www.jetsetmodels.com
- ➢ www.joeedelman.com
- ➢ www.onemodelplace.com
- ➢ www.onetalentsource.com
- ➢ www.models-mart.com
- ➢ www.modelingadvice.com
- ➢ www.modelmingle.com
- ➢ www.modelnetwork.com
- ➢ www.modelsvoice.com
- ➢ www.modelingscams.org
- ➢ www.modellaunch.com
- ➢ www.musecube.com
- ➢ www.newfaces.com
- ➢ www.plusmodels.com
- ➢ www.solomodels.com
- ➢ www.soyouwanna.com
- ➢ www.talentsoup.com
- ➢ www.wilhelmina.com

Another site worth mentioning is myspace.com. Many independent recording artist and filmmakers have used myspace to acquire new fans and reach many industry professionals. I have seen some models use this site to do the same. If you have yet to put up your own site having a myspace page would be of benefit. If you currently have your own site you may use myspace to meet new fans and industry professionals. Some of the great features about myspace is it is free; it allows you to upload a number of pictures, videos and streaming audio. In addition, you could list public appearances in the calendar section. Myspace is currently the most recognized social/business free service site. However, keep your eyes and ears open to the next hot site as you want to ensure you create as many opportunities for yourself as possible. I found that when I share information with the elite I receive information with the elite. When I mention the elite I speak of those who also share valued information. Those that are willing to give of themselves that they too may contribute to the whole and benefit from the sphere of knowledge. I invite you to become one of the elite and share information, contacts and resources found in this book with other aspiring models, their parents and agents.

MODEL PROTECTION

- www.bbb.com
- www.easybackgroundcheck.com
- www.modelingscams.org

MODEL INTERVIEWS

BRAND JOSHUA INTERVIEW

With little to no experience or formal modeling education as a high school student Joshua was at the right place at the right time to secure his first paid modeling assignment. Just a few years later, being at the right place at the right time again secured Joshua another paid modeling contract, this time for a well-established athletic clothing company. Joshua gives his humble opinion on what it takes to become successful as a model. He tells his compelling story of how he was able to secure paid modeling assignments without a modeling agency, management company or photographer referral.

In this interview I ask the who, what, when, why, where and how and Joshua responds candidly. After reading this interview you will know there is more than one way to secure modeling work, if you need comp cards or not, how Joshua got paid what he asked for and advice he gives for new and aspiring models.

Josh how did you get into modeling?

I saw a flyer at the Black College Expo at USC (University of Southern California) for a modeling/casting call. I went to the casting.

What did you do at the casting/modeling call?

I walked up and down the runway. They took my picture and called me back a week later and said would you like to participate as a promotional model.

Were you paid for the event?

Yes, I got paid per event when working with the company.

What is a promotional model?

Someone who promotes a certain brand or company at different events is a promotional model.

How long have you been modeling?

Six years

What type of modeling do you do?

Runway, print and commercial

Josh, as a seasoned model you were able to secure the front cover for Russell Athletics' Team Sport Catalog. Tell me the story of how this came about. What were the actual steps that lead to you securing work as a print model with Russell Athletic?

I was at the gym on a treadmill, training. Andre Murphy of Russell Athletic was in the gym training and asked me have you ever modeled? I told him yes. Then he asked me if I would be interested in a campaign for the Russell Athletic Team Sport Catalog? I told him I was interested. I saw Andre two weeks later at the gym and asked him what was up with the modeling? He said I got you. Andre called me two months later and said are you ready? I told him yeap. He gave me the address to Russell Athletics' Corporate Headquarters to do a fitting. These were the actual steps to securing the Russell Athletic Team Sport Catalog.

What is a fitting in how it relates to your experience with Russell Athletic?

The fitting is where the company took my measurements, I tried on clothes and I was introduced to other people in the Team Sports Division.

How long did the fitting last?

The fitting lasted thirty minutes to an hour.

When did you actually start shooting for the catalog?

Shooting for team sports started the following Monday.

Where did shooting take place?

The shooting took place at the photographer's studio in Atlanta.

Who was the photographer?

Chris Hamilton

How long did the shoot take?

We were shooting four consecutive days for four hours each day.

How did you discuss payment for your modeling services with Russell?

Mr. Murphy asked me how much do you want to get paid? I told him my price and he said ok.

What were the terms of your payment?

I was to get paid after every shoot in the form of a check.

How is it determined how much money models are paid?

Models compensation is based on experience and notoriety in the business.

What did you expect from the shoot?

I expected the shoot to start on time, for the staff to be professional, good food and to get paid at the end of the shoot.

Who was at the shoot?

Me, the photographer, stylist, lighting director and the staff from team sports.

Who typically is at a modeling shoot?

The model, photographer, stylist, make-up artist and whoever is over the project. The stylist may some also be the make up artist at times.

What type of food did they serve you?

In the morning there were beagles, fruit and croissants. During lunch there was Mexican Food.

Do you have comp cards?

No

Did you need comp cards for the Russell Athletic job?

No

Do you need comp cards?

No

Should you have them?

Yes, models should have comp cards. I should have comp cards.

Why should you have comp cards?

Comp cards are models business cards; they are how other people remember you.

What advice would you give to new and aspiring models?

Don't expect people to call you. You must be consistent with going on casting calls. Surround yourself and network with other models. Do work to build your portfolio in the beginning even if you don't get paid. Always be prepared physically and mentally to do what it takes to succeed. Have a sense of humor and personality. Many times people will select a model over someone else simply because they like that model. Having the right personality will take you a long way in this business.

Josh, thank you for your time. How may someone contact you for modeling work, speaking engagements or interviews?

I may be reached at 678-841-3300.

JAWAR SPEAKS WITH NINA ALBARI

I've heard a number of models say modeling schools have not helped their careers. In only a few years after attending modeling school, Nina has become a sought after model, started her own modeling promotions and management company and plans to transition her enterprise into a national brand. While conducting this interview, Nina's assistant was taking calls, scheduling appointments and planning the company's next move. Nina was forthcoming with how she learned about the exclusive modeling business and shares first hand experience about the industry.

In this interview you will learn what a promotional model is, the difference between a modeling agency and modeling manager, how Nina was able to transition her modeling school experience into a growing business and why she doesn't like exclusive contracts with her models.

Have you ever modeled?

Yes

How did you get into modeling business?

I started as a student at Barbizon Modeling School, and then I became a teacher at Barbizon in Charlotte, North Carolina. Next I started Hotgirlz Promotions.

How long have you been modeling?

Five (5) years

What is Hotgirlz Promotions?

Hotgirlz Promotions is an all girl street team and model management company that specializes in getting models work for music videos, print, fashion shows and promotional modeling.

What is a promotional model?

Promotional models promote products, places or things. Their job is to help bring awareness to a product or service.

Why did you start Hotgirlz Promotions?

There were not enough promotions companies in Atlanta where ethnic models could get paid.

How did you start Hotgirlz Promotions?

I started promoting for a clothing line called Hotatlanta. While I was promoting the Hotatlanta Clothing Line I started getting other opportunities to promote for more companies. From then on work would come through referrals.

How many people are on your staff?

Hotgirlz has six (6) staff members and forty-five (45) team members or models.

Will you name some of your past or present clients?

Radio One, Grip Magazine, BME Recordings, Warner Brothers, Uncle Luke [Pioneering Rap Artist & Member of 2 Live Crew], Crunk Energy Drink and Nike, etc.

What sets you apart from other companies?

Hotgirlz Promotions appeals to both urban and corporate clients. We cross-demographics by having access to models of varying ethnicities, sizes and ages. Our models age in range from 18 to 45.

What is the difference between a modeling agency and modeling manager?

An agency automatically takes X number of dollars or percentage from the money a model makes. A model management company helps manage a models career.

Do you have exclusive contracts with your models?

No

Why don't you do exclusivity with a model?

Typically, if an agency or promotions company wants a model to work exclusively for them they will guarantee a model get so much work on a regular basis, since that is their only means of making money as a professional model. I don't want to have to guarantee work for models.

Hotgirlz Models are free to work for a modeling agency or another promotions company. Sometimes we have a lot of work for the models, sometimes we don't. Work is often seasonal and I don't want to keep anyone from making her money.

Were does Hotgirlz Promotions go from hear?

I'm looking at expanding so that we have four major headquarters. We're working on Hotgirlz Promotions North, South, East and West. This will help us better serve our clients.

What do you plan on doing from here?

One of my long-term goals is to offer a full service production house where we offer photography, video, audio and editing. I want to be a one-stop shop for all our clients.

How were you able to get information about the business of modeling?

Through Barbizon Modeling School

What did you learn at Barbizon about the modeling industry?

The first step in being successful is having confidence in yourself. Most people think it is all about being cute, sexy or just physically attractive, but that is only part of it. You have to have confidence. You have to be able to stand in front of the camera, on stage or walk the runway and not be shy. People have to see that you have confidence. The other thing is size does not matter. Most people are only familiar with runway models, which typically are the tall, very thin models, but there are models of all sizes. Plus models make a lot of money, but they have confidence, there not afraid to work in front of the camera or get on stage.

What is the right way to get into the modeling business?

There are some basic things you have to have. You need pictures, comp cards and business cards. You should have different looks with your pictures. Your comp cards should have a casual, fashion and swim wear photos.

What is a comp card?

A comp card is a composite card with versatile looks of a model. A comp card will also have a models weight, height, size, hair color and eye color.

How does a new model get experience?

Work for free, do video shoots, be an extra and build references. You can start adding these references to your resume and they are legit. When you're just getting started you can't be afraid to work for free to build your resume and references. When people see your work effort they will tell other people about you. You have to have a strong work ethic.

What other advice would you give to aspiring models?

Stay focused, you can never have to many pictures-your look will forever change, a good model is versatile, know what your image is and stick to it. If your image is classy, then stick to that image in your work. Don't go trying to look like a seductive model. Like wise if your image is sexy and seductive then stick to that. Focus on what your image is.

Are there any books to read about the modeling business?

No, I can't think of any [modeling business books] off hand. However, I would recommend models read books to help with their face, hair and make-up. You should also read inspiration or self-help books. Modeling is about image, these type of books will help with that. Read magazines that deal with fashion and urban modeling. Watch Americas Top Model, watch and read whatever gives you details about the industry you want to be in. So you can know about the business your in.

Nina you mentioned you have another company, what is it?

Alima Industry, which is a consulting, management, marketing and promotions company dealing with corporate and commercial clients.

How can someone contact you who may be interested in using your services?

My number is 404-558-3036 or 703-508-9195.

MORE MODELING BOOKS

I found it very challenging to find books on the business of modeling in traditional bookstores. Most of the titles below were found through online bookstores. Honestly, I have not read the books below from cover to cover, but thought it would be great to mention them as one of my goals is to ensure the reader has a number of different sources for gathering more information about the business of modeling.

My book was not intended on being the all in one resource guide on the business of modeling. It was intended to be a starting point for someone or anyone knowing someone who was interested in a career in the modeling business in Atlanta who did not have a clue as to the language of the industry or resources to get them started. I challenge the reader to visit the websites mentioned throughout this book to increase their education on the business of modeling.

I would imagine after reading several of the books below you will have a much better appreciation for the business of modeling and how it operates. Perhaps as you read your creative juices will begin to flow allowing you to carve a greater niche in the business. As you read the books below you should research their sources, websites and contacts to increase your knowledge flow on the industry. Sharing your insight with others will help you have a greater command on the business and should position you to meet the right people to help you succeed in the exclusive world of the modeling business. Having a burning desire to achieve your goal, defining success for yourself, creating a practical plan and implementing that plan daily is where you will find the Secrets Revealed to the Modeling Industry.

A Model's Primer
By M. J. Wilson

Atlanta Modeling Industry Secrets Revealed: Resources for Child and Adult Models, Their Agents and Managers
By JaWar

Complete Guide for Models: Inside Advice from Industry Pros for Fashion Modeling
By Eric Bean & Jenni Bidner

Guide to Talent & Modeling Agents
By Rachel Vater

Hand Job: An Insider's Look Into the Modeling Business
By Mike Ramsey

How to Become a Successful Commercial Model: The Complete Commercial Modeling Handbook
By Aaron R. Marcus

Is Modeling for You? The Handbook and Guide for the Young Aspiring Black Model
Author Unknown

Model Scoop and Acting Info
By Eve Matheson

Model and Talent: International Directory of Model & Talent Agencies & Schools
By Gregory James, Jean Walkinshaw

Model Markets of the World
By Marcia Rothschild Moellers

So, You Want to Be a Fashion Model
By Marcia Rothschild Moellers

The Complete Idiot's Guide to Being a Model
By Roshumba Williams with Anne Marie O'Connor

The Truth on Modeling
By Erin Pinckney

Ultimate Plus-Size Modeling Guide
By Catherine Schuller

Wilhelmina Guide to Modeling
By C.I. Walker, Natasha Esch

Your Modeling Career
By Debbie Press

CREATING WEALTH

Whether you earn an additional $5,000 or $5,000,000 a year from the modeling industry, remember to always put a percentage of your earnings (money that you make) aside, preferably in a tax-sheltered account and invest your money in businesses that have nothing to do with the modeling industry. This is called diversification of your assets (money). In addition, you want to always pay yourself first, spend less money than you earn, carry little to no consumer debt and keep accurate and complete records of the money you earn and spend. This will increase your chances for long-term wealth creation and retention. Educate yourself about business and money; after all if you don't mind your business and money, someone else will. To ensure you advance your own learning on saving, investing and creating wealth I have listed a few terms below that you should know.

- **401(k)**
- **Annuities**
- **Assets**
- **Asset Allocation**
- **Bonds**
- **Corporate**
- **Convertible**
- **Government**
- **CD-Certificate Deposit**
- **Checking Account**
- **Compounding Interest**
- **Debt to Income Ratio**
- **Diversification**
- **Dollar-Cost Averaging**

- ➢ **Earnings**
- ➢ **Equity**
- ➢ **Financial Freedom**
- ➢ **Index Funds**
- ➢ **Inflation**
- ➢ **Investment Portfolio**
- ➢ **IRA-Individual Retirement Account**
- ➢ **Keoghs**
- ➢ **Market Index**
- ➢ **Money-Market Accounts**
- ➢ **Money Market Mutual Funds**
- ➢ **NAV (Net Asset Value)**
- ➢ **No-Load Mutual Funds**
- ➢ **Passive Income**
- ➢ **Prospectus**
- ➢ **Real Estate**
- ➢ **Residual Income**
- ➢ **ROI (Return on Investment)**
- ➢ **Roth-IRA, SEP-IRA, Simple-IRA**
- ➢ **Savings Account**
- ➢ **Stocks**
- ➢ **Tax Sheltered Accounts**
- ➢ **Treasury Bill**

Educate yourself about investing and seek the advice of professionals who may help you verify your information. Publications that may help you become familiar with saving and investing your money are Black Enterprise, The Wall Street Journal, Kiplinger, Money, Smart Money, Barron's, Investor Business Daily, Financial Times, the Business Section of the Atlanta Journal Constitution and the Money Section of USA Today. Think and Grow Rich by Napolean Hill, The Richest Man in Babylon, Rich Dad Poor Dad and Black & Green are books that will help you learn how the mind of money works. After you read them, reread them a few times over and begin to execute the information found in them, as you do so you will witness changes in your own thinking, planning and carefully crafted execution. For more information on saving, investing and making your money grow; visit the following websites.

www.bankrate.com
www.blackenterprise.com
www.buyandhold.com
www.creditinfocenter.com
www.fool.com
www.indexfunds.com
www.investoreducation.org
www.jumpstartcoalition.org
www.kiplinger.com
www.marketwatch.com
www.mfea.com

www.money.com
www.moneyopolis.org
www.moringstar.com
www.richdadpoordad.com
www.rothira.com
www.smartmoney.com
www.tiaacref.com
www.troweprice.com
www.youdecide.com
www.vanguard.com

THINK

PLAN

EXECUTE

VISUALLY STIMULATING THE
WAY YOU'RE PERCEIVED...
DESIGN APART
Urban & Corporate design
album covers
demo cd/mixed tapes
logos
business cards
promotional posters
t-shirts
professional photography
club flyers
404_351+4312 | designashil@yahoo.com

MUSIC INDUSTRY CONNECTION

by
JAWAR

LOS ANGELES MUSIC INDUSTRY Connection

Resources For:

ARTISTS
PRODUCERS
MANAGERS

BY

JAWAR

EBS
Entertainment Business Support
ATLANTA • GA
Ph. 404.217.0696
email. kfennell@entertainmentbizsupport.com
web. www.entertainmentbizsupport.com

ABOUT THE AUTHOR
JAWAR

Chief Visionary Officer of Music Therapy 101, a Music Business Conference since 1998, has given informative seminars in Atlanta, Los Angeles and Washington D.C. He created the workshop to identify and share vital information in a step-by-step process necessary for success and ultimate longevity in the music biz with aspiring artists and those willing to be involved in the music industry.

In 2002, JaWar created the MIC (Music Industry Connection) one of the few free all Music Business Publications that serves all genres of music. In just over a year the MIC tripled is circulation, doubled its' page count and increased its' subscription base. When your event demands practical, relevant, and useful information from an enthusiastic speaker who has legitimately "been there" by releasing the Dark Ages II & Paranormal Activity CDs on his independent record company Kemetic Records consider JaWar; he may be contacted at 800-963-0949, jawar@mt101.com or P.O. Box 52682, Atlanta, GA 30355, USA.

JaWar provides business consulting services with an emphasis on branding, marketing & promotions, strategic planning and profit increasing to select businesses and individuals seeking to advance their companies goals and objectives. Whether through one-on-one consultation or in a business group setting, JaWar may help your business become more efficient and effective.